Where Do Animals Live?

by Linette Ellis Mathewson

MONDO

Photo Credits:

Cover and Pages 3, 12: © Craig Tuttle/Corbis Stock Market; Title Page: © David Boyle/Earth Scenes; Page 4: © Rob & Ann Simpson; Pages 5, 16 (left): © Francis Lepine/Animals Animals; Pages 6, 9, 11, 15, 16 (center): © E. R. Degginer/Animals Animals; Page 7: © Don Enger/Animals Animals; Page 8: © Michael Gadomski/ Earth Scenes; Page 10: © Brian Miller/Animals Animals; Pages 13, 16 (right): © O.S. F./Animals Animals; Page 14: © S. Morris, O.S.F./Animals Animals

Text copyright © 2004 by MONDO Publishing

For information contact:
MONDO Publishing
980 Avenue of the Americas
New York, NY 10018

Visit our web site at http://www.mondopub.com

Printed in China

04 05 06 07 08 09   9 8 7 6 5 4 3 2 1

ISBN 1-58653-971-X
Designed by Jean Cohn

Contents

What Lives in a Tree?

This is a tree. Do animals live in trees? Yes! Animals live in trees.

What animal do you see in this tree?
An owl is in this tree.

What animal do you see in this tree?
A squirrel is in this tree.

What animal do you see in this tree?
An eagle is in this tree.

What Lives in a Pond?

This is a pond. Do animals live in ponds? Yes! Animals live in ponds.

What animal do you see in this pond?
A frog is in this pond.

What animal do you see in this pond?
A turtle is in this pond.

What animal do you see in this pond?
A fish is in this pond.

What Lives in the Ground?

This is the ground. Do animals live in the ground? Yes! Animals live in the ground.

What animal do you see in the ground?
A rabbit is in the ground.

What animal do you see in the ground?
A spider is in the ground.

What animal do you see in the ground?
A worm is in the ground.

Where do animals live?
They live in trees. They live in ponds.
They live in the ground.